GATEWAY to TUTORING

Written By:

Char Geletka

&

Karen Hunter

DEDICATION

This book is dedicated to our amazingly supportive husbands - and our children who inspired our love of tutoring.

CONTENTS

Let's
Talk
About
the
Basics

Let's Talk About the Basics

Introduction

Welcome! We are so glad you're here!

Tutoring is an exceptional business that offers you the opportunity to:

- Be an entrepreneur - be your own boss!

- Earn as much money as you want

- Make a difference in the lives of others (that could use your help)

- Make your own hours

- Make extra income as a side job or full-time career

- Inspire others to succeed

How could you ask for a better career?!

You're earning great money and inspiring students – one at a time!

In all of our years of tutoring, we've *never* grown weary or burned out. We love touching the lives of others, helping students and parents achieve their goals, and have the satisfaction of being in control of our careers.

As you read through this manual to help you start your tutoring business, you'll see: We *LOVE what we do!* Tutoring is an engaging and inspiring business that you can begin slowly or jump in with both feet.

Tutors are in high demand and the ever-growing need for tutoring makes this the best time for you to get started!

We value your time and appreciate your choice to pick up this book. With that in mind, we don't want to waste your time with a bunch of fluff as you read through this "how to" book, so we've tried to keep our methods concise and to the point.

About Us

We want to make the most of your time as you read but thought you may like to know a little about us - if not, you can move on to the next section.

We both eased our way into tutoring and firmly believe that is the best way to start. Each student teaches you something about tutoring, about yourself, and about the skills you will need to be the best tutor in town. And that's our goal! We don't want to you to have a mediocre tutoring business - we want you to have the reputation of being the best at what you do and rock that "Best Tutor in Town" badge!

So how did we start? Believe it or not, we were both homeschooling moms with professional backgrounds.

Starting from the time Char's children were kindergarten age she taught her two boys until the 9th and 11th grades. Karen taught her son through 8th grade, as well, and continues to homeschool her daughter, who is now a senior in high school. For three years Karen also taught at a private school.

Throughout our homeschooling years we wrote curriculum, taught classes in homeschool co-op settings, and passed along the love of learning to many children. This experience was rewarding in many ways. When we found we had more time on our hands as our children grew older, we offered our services to others and began down the path to becoming private tutors.

First, we started with one student and then another and another... until our businesses grew!

Oh boy, did we learn a lot!

We already understood learning styles and teaching methods, but there was so much more to learn.

That's why we wrote this book - to make it easier for you.

Karen has a degree in Accounting, and Char has a degree in Finance. After tutoring for a few years, Char went on to earn her Master's Degree in Education.

Don't be afraid to take some classes or seminars that can help you hone your skills. The more prepared you feel, the more confident you will be with your student. Confidence is key!

Over the years as our client base grew, we'd find ourselves

cheering each other on...

"How many students do you have?"

"How much money are you making?"

We would also encourage each other and suggest resources when presented with a challenging situation.

It's been an incredibly exciting journey to do something we absolutely love and get paid for it! Which is why we want to share our discoveries with you.

Along with this manual, you can find additional information on our website, <u>GatewayToTutoring.com</u>.

Enough about us...let's get to the nitty gritty and get you in business!

Tutor Tip:

For Additional Information visit:

GatewaytoTutoring.com

So, Why Tutor?

Tutoring is big business. There will always be students that need help and parents that want their students to succeed.

Even Olympians have coaches, don't they?!

If you love learning, love inspiring others, and love making money...tutoring could be the golden nugget to bring you great rewards - emotionally and financially.

It's a win-win business!

Tutoring in the US is a $7 billion industry. The top 50 US tutoring franchises comprise only 30% of this. Franchises include companies such as Sylvan Learning and Mathnasium. The majority of tutoring services are privately owned and are expected to grow 7% each year through 2022. We have to believe the numbers are higher due to the fact that some tutors may not report their income.

The reason for this growth is largely due to the increasing number of students enrolling in universities and colleges. Parents and their students are looking for help to meet education standards and increase their grades to better prepare them.

You have knowledge that can be shared with others!

Whether you have an engineering background, raised or are raising children, have obtained a college degree or are in the process of earning one, worked in an office, are a veteran of the Armed Forces, worked at a hobby you enjoy, tinker with computers, program software professionally or are self-taught, are bilingual, are a history buff, or *so much more...* you can teach others.

All of the experiences and knowledge that you have acquired can be passed along to others who have not risen to the level you have. And yes, you probably don't know it all - but that's okay.

If you're willing to sharpen some skills that will help you to convey what you already know, and are willing to continue learning, tutoring is for you!

What would it feel like to have freedom from punching a clock or working bell to bell?

What is that freedom worth to you?

Do you enjoy inspiring others?

Quite likely you already have many of the skills you need in order to start tutoring.

This book will help you know how to develop the skills you have, pair those skills with your desire to tutor, and give you the confidence to begin tutoring tomorrow!

Why Tutor?!

- Tutoring is a $7 billion business
- Flexible Hours
- Great Pay

Skills That Will Make You Successful

Listening –

Listening is key! It is important to listen to the concerns and desires of the parents as well as students. Parents know the strengths and weaknesses of their child better than anyone and often use the services of a tutor to get their child from point A to point B. Listening to students carefully, along with their body language and tone, will convey vital information. Occasionally a student will tell you that they understand the material yet, show hesitancy. The best way of confirming this is to ask them to explain the idea, concept, or steps to you in their own words. Listening beyond their, "Yeah, I get it," will help you fill in the gaps.

Adaptability –

Perhaps you learned a particular way when you were in school. For example, you sat in a quiet room, with a desk, and no calculator. But in this day and age, being adaptable as a tutor is vital. You want to be in sync with new technology, new teaching methods, and learning styles. For example, Common Core, which is the set of standards that most public-school curriculum is aligned with, has methods of teaching that you may not be familiar with. (More on how to find information on Common Core is discussed in Section Two). It is extremely important that you are able to support how the material is addressed in class so you know how to adapt your approach to the tutoring session. Be ready!

Flexibility –

Sometimes a parent or student will need to make a change in their schedule. We try not to be so overbooked that we cannot accommodate them when the need arises. This will enhance your value and will make your clients more understanding when you may need to shift a session yourself.

Always be the one that gives more than your client expects.

If they cancel a session at the last minute for a *good* reason- don't charge them. If that continues, well, you'll need to charge them in order for them to respect you as a professional.

Positivity –

Having a positive and optimistic attitude conveys hope and is essential to every tutoring session. Students often draw strength from the confidence that their tutor has in them. For example, if you're troubled by the teacher, the curriculum, or the teaching methods, don't let it show. Talk privately with the parents or email the teacher for clarification. It's important to remember: when a student tells you something that doesn't sound quite right.... there's probably some information missing!

Patience –

Every so often, a student needs to have a new concept explained multiple ways before they begin to grasp it. Staying calm and keeping a pleasant demeanor throughout the process is key.

Remember that often, the parents have hired you because they don't want to push through the frustration and/or manipulation from their children. Don't think for a minute that their children won't try antics with you! You being able to handle the students seamlessly in these times of manipulation makes you *PRICELESS!*

Creativity –

From learning a math algorithm ... to memorizing a new vocabulary word, presenting a concept in a different manner than what you have been using can often help the student become proficient with it in a short amount of time. In other words - don't be afraid to change it up!

Be willing to try new methods or take a different approach to material based on their specific learning style. (Learning styles are discussed in Section Four). Try having the student teach the lesson, use manipulatives for math, or create a song.

These techniques do not have to be uniquely your own ideas - though they might! An internet search can reveal oodles of ways you can enhance a lesson with a little creativity.

The Best Tutors Are:

- Good Listeners
- Positive
- Adaptable
- Patient
- Flexible
- Creative

Let's Get Started!

Let's Get Started

Business Models

You can offer your tutoring services in different ways. Here are three of the most common:

Employee –

You can become an employee of a tutoring center where students are provided to you. The advantages to this is that you will not need to market your services to find clients. If you're not excited about marketing yourself, this may be the best choice for you. A disadvantage of working for an agency is that the center pays you an hourly fee. Examples include Mathnasium, Kumon, and Sylvan Learning to name a few.

Tutoring Service Subcontractor –

You can connect with clients through a tutoring service online or a tutoring service in your area.

Again, the major advantage is that you will not need to find your own clients, they are directed to you. The disadvantage is that these types of services keep a portion of the fees. An example of a web-based business is Wyzant.com.

Private Tutor –

Lastly, you can market yourself and become a private, home-based provider. The advantage is that you keep one hundred percent of the fees you charge. The disadvantage, or challenge, is that you must find your own students.

Tutor Tip:

3 Ways to Structure Your Tutoring Business

- Employee
- Tutoring Contractor
- Private Tutor - Self Employed

Tutor What You're Passionate About

One of the most important decisions you make will be "what" subjects to tutor. Our best advice to you is to tutor the subjects that you are passionate about, especially when you are starting out. For Char, that's writing and reading comprehension. Karen loves math! It's a good practice to always have names of other tutors that you can refer clients to that satisfy the subjects that you cannot/don't care to tutor. This will position you as a resource for your clients as they spread the news that they know an amazing tutor *(i.e., you!)*

If you take on a subject that you are less than excited about, your student will sense that you are just another teacher. As a tutor your goal should be to not only teach the material but inspire your students so they become excited about learning.

Our personal goal is always to build our students confidence and ignite a love of learning in each of our students.

It is an exciting day when you see a desire in your students to learn beyond the lessons they are required to complete!

As a tutor, you want to see an excitement in your students - where they research and learn more than is required because you've helped to become them interested in the subjects. This doesn't come easily to reluctant learners which is why we encourage you to exhibit an eagerness for the material as you teach.

Your enthusiasm is contagious and will help to relieve any anxiety that your student feels.

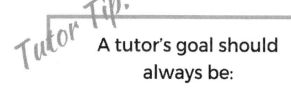

A tutor's goal should always be:

- Build their student's confidence
- Ignite a love of learning

Identifying Subjects to Tutor

If you're not sure what subjects you are qualified to teach you can start with your favorite! This will ensure that you will be willing to learn as you grow with your students. Understand that the education model has many fast - moving parts and knowing everything there is to know about a subject is not possible. Just when you think you know it all - the standards are rewritten - as happened with Common Core standards!

Thank goodness that your students don't expect you to be perfect or an expert in every subject.

However, if you promote yourself as an expert in a subject - you should be! Or you will be exposed.

If you're still not sure about which subjects to tutor, visit Wyzant.com and sign up to be a tutor. One of the wonderful features of the site is the qualification tests that are required for each tutor. These tests assure students that their tutor is qualified and knowledgeable to tutor in each subject that they advertise. As a tutor, it will help you narrow down the areas that you are comfortable with.

We strongly suggest you take these assessments. Not only will they help you to determine your level of expertise, but also your interest in each of the subjects. As you take the tests, if you find yourself getting frustrated or searching the internet for answers, you may want to forego that subject. You don't have to activate your account on Wyzant prior to taking the assessments, so if you don't want to tutor through Wyzant, you aren't committed.

Subjects You Can Tutor

- Reading
- Math
- English
- Science
- History
- Foreign Language
- Government
- Test Prep
- Writing
- Music Theory
- Art
- Computers

Be A Step Ahead

This one piece of advice will help you build your reputation faster than any other strategy:

Tutor subjects you are passionate and excited about.

For example, when potential clients ask you what subjects you tutor in, tell them, "I can tutor in all subjects except upper level math and science." The subjects you are not comfortable tutoring, you can refer clients to a tutor who is much more savvy and excited about them.

You don't want to commit yourself to tutoring a subject that you will dread or you don't have the time to invest in. This will be laborious and ultimately won't do your student any favors.

However, if you're up for a challenge... ***Go for it!***

Remember, if you delve into a subject or area that you are not entirely familiar with, you must be willing to put in the work to stay ahead of your clients.

Char: After I had been tutoring for a few years one of my clients asked me to open a learning center for homeschool middle school aged gifted students. I was excited about the opportunity and dove right in! This meant nonstop research, writing curriculum, hiring and training teachers in project-based learning methods, and more! I loved it, but it required an immense amount of work. I remember thinking that it took all my effort to stay one step ahead of the teachers, the sponsors and the students because managing a learning center was new to me. And sometimes I felt like I was a full 1/2 step ahead! But I was still ahead! And that's what matters!

You must stay ahead of your students and parents.

Likewise, if you have a client that wants you to tutor in a multi-subject capacity, you must be willing to put in the work.

Char: From the first phone call, one of my clients explained that he was looking for an everyday/long-term tutor - one who will tutor all subjects for several years. I was honest with him and told him that I love reading, writing, organization and math. Science wasn't my favorite and I wouldn't exclusively tutor science, but as homework help, I can certainly handle it and get excited about it. I explained that it is my policy to only tutor subjects that I love so that I can pass on a love of learning to my students. Parents appreciate your honesty. **And so do students!**

If you find yourself tutoring a subject that is beyond your expertise, don't despair!

You are obviously a smart cookie if you've decided to tutor. At this point you have two choices - push through and study ahead of each session or find another tutor for your student. This is what you can do for advanced math for example.

> *Char:* I love math! It was my favorite subject in school. It's black and white and so am I! But I'm rusty. Rather than study a whole math book prior to each session that's far beyond my current comfort level, I pass my math students on to Karen - who specializes in math. Understand, I do have math students, but I brush up on the material, (if I'm rusty) each week before I see them, to be sure I am comfortable with the lesson.

Being stretched by a lesson or a tricky question is something that will happen to everyone from time to time - if you are tutoring above sixth grade level. Be honest. But don't let it happen too often. What we mean is...if you find yourself, time and time again, fumbling and panicking because you don't know the material - you are probably not the best choice in tutors for the student in that subject. Always put the student's need for a solid education ahead of your desire to make money.

If you run across a problem/question that you don't know how to solve, utilize the internet. Quite likely, the answer or methods you need, are available to help you in a crunch. YouTube videos are great at these moments too.

> *Char:* One student sprung factorials and permutations on me, which, unfortunately, only looked vaguely familiar that day. He didn't understand them, and I didn't understand them, so I pulled out my cell phone and picked out what looked like an easy and short video - and we learned together. It took less than five minutes, and we were on our way to completing his homework.

Using your cell phone as a tool is a wonderful example to your student who is probably using it more as a toy.

Smartphones are a wonderful resource. Don't be afraid to use it. As a general rule, you should keep your cell phone on silent and out of view, but when the occasion warrants, you may want to pull it out.

If your student's parent walks in the room when you have your phone out, casually mention what you are looking up so that they know you aren't texting during your session.

Parents will appreciate that you are going the extra mile to help their student.

Tutor Tip:

Always stay a step ahead of your student.

Put in the time necessary to be an

expert in the subjects you tutor

Get Familiar with Common Core

Though some educators don't care for Common Core, it is not going anywhere. Plain and simple there has been too much money, time, and effort spent implementing it to consider that the developmental levels or methods need to be adjusted. As tutors, we need to be familiar with Common Core standards and methods being taught.

You aren't sure what Common Core is?

Here is the definition from CommonCore.org website:

> The Common Core is a set of high-quality academic standards in mathematics and English language arts/ literacy (ELA). These learning goals outline what a student should know and be able to do at the end of each grade. The standards were created to ensure that all students graduate from high school with the skills and knowledge necessary to succeed in college, career, and life, regardless of where they live. Forty-one states, the District of Columbia, four territories, and the Department of Defense Education Activity (DoDEA) have voluntarily adopted and are moving forward with the Common Core. (from commoncore.org)

In short, the standards are a nifty idea. They were set to ensure that, regardless of where you live in the US, your student will be on the same educational track as other students throughout the country. Moving from one region to another wouldn't affect your student's ability to assimilate into a school. And ultimately, having one blanket standard would assure each student's success and readiness for college, career, and life.

Sounds like a winner, right?! How could they go wrong?

Well, if you've had any exposure to Common Core math - you might know. Their methodology is incredibly different and involves more steps than anyone needs to solve a math problem! But *(sigh)*, it's here to stay - at least for a while.

Be sure to keep a positive attitude toward the school's methodology to best help your student.

Understand that many teachers tell their students to NOT let their parents help them with their math homework because parents try to teach the old methods (which are easier). Typically, parents don't take the time to learn the new methods. That's where your value as an informed tutor will skyrocket.

Familiarize yourself with Common Core standards and how the strategies are taught in your student's

curriculum.

When the methods are new and confusing to parents, they will appreciate your expertise in an area that baffles them.

Although most private school students are not learning Common Core methods, public school students are.

Where do you start? How much do you need to know? If you teach math, it's important that you take time to educate yourself with the new methods that are being taught which are *VERY* different from anything we learned in school. Research. Learn.

You don't want to be caught off guard and find yourself not understanding how to help a 4th grader multiply 3-digit equations. Be forewarned! *This will happen if you don't take the time to learn the new methods.* Don't let that scare you - the methods are not difficult, they are simply different. And quite different!

If you find yourself in a situation where your student needs help and you don't know how to help them with the new methods - *do not, do n-o-t*, teach them your old way. Sure, it may be better/easier/more logical, but it is very disrespectful to the school (and the parent's investment in you) to teach a method that will ultimately not help the student succeed in the classroom.

Your job is to transform your student into a confident and successful student. Don't forget the goal!

A wonderful resource to learn all you ever want to know about Common Core can be found at this website:

https://www.edutopia.org/common-core-state-standards-resources

Be sure to take some time and familiarize yourself with your state standards. Do this by watching videos, joining a forum, or signing up for a newsletter.

Tutor Tip:

Always seek to be an authority on what's going on in the schools.

This will continue to make you valuable!

Keeping Records

We recommend using the easiest method possible to record your income, expenses, and mileage.

The easier it is, the more likely you are to keep up with it!

You don't need fancy software or ledger books. When you begin tutoring buy a small lined blank journal.

Every time you receive a fee, record the date, the amount, the client, and if it was paid in cash write "Cash" or if paid by check record the check number. You should also note where it was so that you can keep track of the mileage for tax purposes.

For example:

1/23/2013   Johnny $100   Ck#1208   Library

About two-thirds into the book place a paperclip to begin your recording the expenses you incur while tutoring. This includes supplies, copying fees, business cards and the like. Record the date of the purchase, the vendor, the amount, and the purpose. Place all receipts in a folder or an envelope in chronological order as you accrue them.

At the end of the year, you can combine the income, the expenses, and miles for your tax return. We recommend you hire an accountant for specific advice or questions you may have. At the beginning of a new year, begin with a new journal.

If a journal doesn't work for you, try using the note section in your smartphone or a cloud-based document like Google Drive that you can access from your phone or computer. Make it convenient.

The key is to make record keeping doable.

That might sound a bit oversimplified, but if you find a system that you can easily keep up with, you will thank yourself at the end of the year. Whatever system works for you is the system that you should use. Just be sure to be thorough.

The last thing you want to do is go back through a year and recreate your income, expenses, and mileage. If your business is thriving this will not only be a project you don't have time for, you will miss opportunities for write-offs.

> *Karen:* I deposit checks electronically to my bank account from my phone. Once I've made the deposit, I make a large check mark across the front of it and write the date. These also go into my expense folder for the year. If ever there is a question about a payment it is easy to find the check number

and/or amount.

Also, one of my clients requested receipts for each check. I have a template on my writing program that I can quickly fill in and email her the receipt in a PDF format each week. I find that when I use templates and have a simple system, it is easy to keep records up-to-date. We have included a printable invoice template for you to use in the Resource section of our website at www.gatewaytotutoring.com.

Tutor Tip:

Make Record Keeping as Simple as Possible!

No one wants to go back and recreate a
years of expenses!
You will miss write-offs

Insurance

Although tutoring is a low-risk profession, it may be a good idea to have extra coverage just in case the unexpected happens.

If you see students in your own home, you may be covered with personal liability insurance. This covers bodily injury and property damage sustained by others for whom you are legally responsible.

We recommend that you contact your insurance company to be certain! Also, check with your agent to see if they recommend additional coverage. Usually the cost is minimal.

If you tutor students in your home, their home, or at a public location such as a library, you might consider getting General Liability (GL) coverage. GL protects you from a variety of claims: bodily injury, property damage, personal injury and the like.

Another type of insurance is Professional Liability which protects you if you ever sued for not doing a good job. (Sounds crazy, but we live in America where people sue for just about anything, so this is available as well). Insurance options are unique to each individual - so again, we recommend that you speak to your current agent and go from there.

The National Tutoring Association offers insurance to its members at a group rate, which is something to keep in mind if you are looking for GL coverage.

Tutor Tip:

Insurance

Contact your insurance agent to find out what coverage is best for your business.

Marketing

Marketing is the elephant in the room that everyone is concerned about. Plain and simple, to find tutoring jobs you will need to get your name out there.

Business cards and flyers are tools that work very well.

Having a professional looking business card available to hand to out is a must!

You never know when you might come across someone who is interested in tutoring for their child or knows someone who is looking for a tutor.

> *Karen*: There have been many times I have struck up conversations with people while out running errands and after learning that I tutor, they have asked for my card. Leads can come from many places and often unexpectedly. Once, I met a woman sitting next to me at the nail salon while getting a pedicure and it turned out she was a distributor for a major education publisher. She said she was always coming across people looking for tutors and would love to get my card. Thank goodness I had one! I always make sure I have some neatly tucked into my phone case since my cell phone

undoubtedly goes everywhere I do.

Business cards should have your name, phone number, email address and state/region that you tutor. If you want to market to a specific aspect of tutoring such as test preparation or high school math, you can add that detail. We recommend you have them printed at an office supply store or a similar type business. Home printed cards usually look like they are home-made. Keep the cards clean and unbent; they are a reflection of you.

Here are some online resources you can use to design your professional business cards:

- Canva.com

- Vistaprint.com

- Moo.com

- Staples/Office Depot - you can design cards and pick them up in 12 hours for under $20!

- And so many more....

But why go crazy?! Just get a card and distribute it! If you don't like it in a month, don't be afraid to change it up and reprint for less than $20! Don't be cheap when it comes to spending money to make money!

Another smart marketing tool is a business flyer. Again, these need to be professional looking. Add color, different fonts, and the like to grab your reader's attention. Carefully consider the type of graphics, words, and pictures - and design it accordingly. The flyers should not be too wordy but clearly state the subjects you tutor in and how a person can contact you. There are many things vying for our attention these days. If you are like us, what we spend time reading must grab our interest rather quickly.

When you advertise, whether it be through flyers or ads, always put yourself in the place of the potential customer.

Define the need that you are meeting (i.e., the problem you are solving), and design your marketing materials accordingly.

Never hesitate to tell others what you do! Let them feel your enthusiasm and excitement for tutoring! Even if you don't have your first "official" student yet, tell others that you are a tutor. This can be true even if you currently don't have any official students. Have you helped your own child, a friend, a relative, or a neighbor with a homework problem? If so, you can answer honestly.

> *Karen:* I can't ever remember someone ever drilling me about how long I've tutored...or how many students I have! I remember meeting my first student and her mom some years

ago. The mom was much more interested in the fact that I was flexible with my scheduling and that I showed an interest in her eight-year-old daughter more than anything. I still tutor her today.

With the internet, opportunity is just a click away! You can promote yourself on Facebook, Instagram or LinkedIn. Don't overlook the obvious - your friends that know you and trust you. Create a Facebook Event or a Facebook Live to introduce your business.

Other places you can promote your tutoring services:

- Wyzant.com

- Superprof.com

- Care.com

- Homeschooling Organizations

- Schools

- Libraries

- Craigslist

- Start a blog/website

Volunteering to tutor someone who needs homework help is a great way to get your feet wet. This will also help you determine the areas you'd like to specialize in.

There is a plethora of volunteering opportunities with tutoring children. This can be found at a local library or literacy coalition; even classrooms welcome the help!

Offering your services for free helps build confidence and shows your genuine desire to help others.

> *Karen:* I volunteer at my church to tutor students who live nearby and who could not otherwise afford it. Though I started doing this after I had become an established tutor, this is a great way to gain experience, and give back to the community at the same time.

Homeschooling is a market that should not be missed.

Market your services through co-ops, in newsletters, at curriculum fairs. Both of us have taught classes to small homeschool groups. Charging a minimal fee per student/class, becomes a nice hourly rate. Often you will find a homeschool parent who isn't comfortable in a particular subject and looks for outside help, and this is where you come in! This is your opportunity to get your name out there.

Once you are known as a tutor, referrals are a great way to expand your business.

Referrals from one parent to another often happen naturally, but don't be afraid to ask if you are looking to expand.

If you're a tutor whom a parent has come to know and trust, they are   more than happy to tell others about you. Your clients who know you and your work ethic will be excited to help you succeed.

Tutor Tip:

Marketing your Tutoring Services can happen anywhere!

- Distribute Business Cards & Flyers
- Post on Social Media about your Tutoring
- Advertise online
- Create a profile on Wyzant or Superprof

Pricing

The pricing of your tutoring sessions depends on a few factors:

- The subjects you tutor – and grade level

- Your experience

- What does your market warrant?

- Are you in a more elite area?

- Or are you tutoring homeschoolers who struggle financially?

Perhaps you want to tutor in various demographics. Upper level math and science tutors tend to make more than reading and writing tutors as a general rule.

As your reputation builds and your schedule fills, you will quite likely want to raise your rates. Be very sensitive as to how you handle this in your community where you rely on a good reputation and word of mouth referrals. That can become a little tricky if you are charging similar customers different rates. You have the option to raise your rates across the board for all of your clients. Or you might like to exempt your customers that you've tutored for many years – and keep them at the lower price they began with.

If, by chance, your clients know each other (or are in the same social circles around town), be honest with the lower paying clients and let them know you've raised your rates and ask them not to share your rate with others.

We have provided a printable invoice template for you at our website www.gatewaytotutoring.com.

You never want to offend a client over a few dollars.

Tutor Tip:

How to Price Your Tutoring Services

- What does your market warrant?
- What subject are you tutoring?
- What grade level are you tutoring?

Let's Get Up & Running!

Let's Get Up & Running!

Your First Point of Contact

It is important to present yourself as a professional from the very first phone call. We recommend you don't answer your phone from an unfamiliar number unless you have a pen or pencil in hand. It's better to miss a phone call from a potential client than to pick up the phone and only remember a fraction of the information the parent gave you.

That first phone call is very, very important. That is your interview.

Be prepared or don't pick up the phone. Preparation includes having your sales pitch ready.

Char: I remember one parent asking me point-blank, "So, what do you do?"

What do I do?! I tutor!!!

46

I fumbled a little and began explaining how I look for the student's learning style and nervously explained how I establish a solid relationship with my students to help build their confidence and make sure they understand that I am on their team. Thankfully, that satisfied my caller! But I learned a valuable lesson that day...

Every tutor must have a very clear, concise answer to explain their teaching philosophy and methods.

Tutor Tip: Have a three minute elevator pitch ready so that you can confidently explain:
- How you tutor,
- Your philosophy,
- Your strengths, and
- What sets you apart from other tutors.

Information to Gather

From the very first phone call you should gather pertinent information about your student and your client's expectations.

Here are some helpful topics to discuss:

- The student's name, age and grade

- The name of the school that the student attends

- The parent's concerns about the student's academic performance

- Are there any behavioral issues?

- How is the communication between the parent and the school/teacher?

- Has the student ever worked with a tutor in the past? If so, what were the strategies that were tried and were they successful?

- Always be sure to discuss the location, pricing and scheduling during the first phone call.

- Arrange a time and place to meet.

Remember to write down the information you gather. It is easy to forget pertinent information that your client will assume you remember. Consider too, that when you do remember important details, your client will appreciate your attention to his child.

Additionally, you can ask the parent to fill out a questionnaire to provide details about their child. This is helpful as they will provide insight that may help you in your time with the child

A Parent Questionnaire is included in the Resource section of our website www.gatewaytotutoring.com.

Tutor Tip:

Get to Know Your Client

From the first conversation, take notes and ask specific questions

What to Wear

Another very simple yet effective, way of presenting yourself as a professional is how you dress. Do you know that old phrase, "Dress for the job you want?"

If you want to be considered a professional, and you want to be paid like a professional, you should dress like a professional.

We have seen tutors dress in shorts, gym clothes, and the like and wonder: *How much can they get paid? Do their clients respect their abilities? Do they take their job seriously?*

It is important to consider the message you are sending with your appearance and demeanor. Remember who your client is - typically it is your student's parent, and quite likely if they have the money to pay for tutoring, they are professionals and expect you to be as well.

Remember human nature is a factor. It is more natural to respect and listen to someone who presents themselves as a professional in their appearance.

Obviously, dressing nicer doesn't make you more capable but it certainly doesn't hurt to gain a little more favor with your clients just by dressing up a bit. They are your employer.

Dress Like a Professional

Your appearance makes an impact
on how your client sees you

Your First Meeting

The first time we meet a parent and student the session is always complementary. It does not make sense to charge for a meeting when personalities might not align or schedules might not work out. Although you attempt to get pertinent information during the initial phone call, sometimes meeting in person will reveal details that make it impractical to work with the student. Offering this one-time session for free will avoid uncomfortable situations if the relationship doesn't continue.

During the phone call when you arrange the meeting, you should ask the parent to have curriculum and school work examples available for you to review. This will give you a feel for the level of work that is required and the student's aptitude.

When you meet the student for the first time, it's important to be friendly and encouraging. Let them know you're looking forward to working together and determine the parent's goals for tutoring.

Take time and go through the examples of the school work in their curriculum and binders that they present to you, and ask the student questions to involve them.

Interacting with the student will also give you a feel for how cooperative he or she is and establish a much-needed rapport. This is your opportunity to set the parent and student at ease. Also, taking time to look at their school work will be invaluable as you work with them to identify their strengths and weaknesses.

First Impressions

- Be Friendly & Professional
- Review the Student's Work
- Establish goals with the parent

Learning Environment

The environment in which you choose to tutor your student is crucial to the success you will experience during your tutoring sessions. It's almost as important as your qualifications. If you choose the wrong environment, the whole session could end up being a waste of your time, your student's time, and your client's money.

> *Char:* One of my students had a germ anxiety and was convinced that the library was full of pathogens, but the local coffee shop was not. We met several times at the library and wiped down the desk in the study room, and he did fine. I'm not sure how it happened, or why I agreed to it, but we eventually met in a coffee shop – oh, big mistake! For an adolescent boy, the distractions were too much. Urging him through each exercise, while drawing his attention back to the lesson constantly, we "successfully" finished his lesson. But I learned a lesson myself that day! Coffee shops will not work for most students. Perhaps adults and college students, but not children.

A quiet place is imperative. Not because you need total quiet during a tutoring session – but because you should be in control of your environment.

The more distractions, the less likely you will be able to effectively pilot how the session goes.

Our favorite place to tutor is in the students' homes. Students are most comfortable in their own home, and you can easily fit into their world as long as you have a quiet place to work.

Additionally, you are likely to have the parent's support if you need it. And if you run into a glitch and need extra time, students will usually have a little cushion in their schedule if they're meeting at home. That almost guarantees you won't have to cut off a lesson in the middle of an explanation (because mom is texting from the parking lot that she's waiting for her child).

Another benefit to tutoring the child at home is the convenience of their schoolwork. There's usually a place where old homework, tests, and relevant papers end up. If not in the bottom of the backpack, then probably the corner of the desk where they do their homework - *at home.*

One of the advantages to tutoring is the ability to be flexible. You can meet in a library, at your student's home, and in other locations. When your hourly rate is significant you can rationalize traveling a little to make it convenient for your clients.

A number of tutors work out of their own house and have four to six students back-to-back. That works well if you can keep that pace. Lining up tutoring sessions in this manner works best when you are tutoring a single subject and don't need to switch curriculum and subjects. This works well for teachers who tutor students after school hours.

Details you should consider if you are having students tutor in your home:

- How will this affect your family?

- Do you have pets and do your students have allergies to pets?

- You might want to have a sitting room where parents can wait.

Libraries, study rooms, and conference rooms are other locations that may work well for you.

However, if you want to present yourself as a professional, you will want to act professional.

That means meeting in a place that commands your student's attention and gives you the floor – without distractions, which is almost certainly a home or a library.

At the beginning, as you're building your business, you may be so excited to have a student that you agree to an environment like a coffee shop. If that happens and you find out it doesn't work, be honest with your client and let them know, but be sure to suggest a specific alternative as a solution. They will appreciate that you care about their child's learning.

However, it is best to set your standards from the start so that both you and your student will do well.

Pick a quiet place, have control of the atmosphere and make it an engaging and positive place to learn.

Tutor Tip:

Where to Tutor

The best place to meet is a place that commands your student's attention and gives you the floor – without distractions.

Tools - Pack Your Bag

As a tutor, you want to be prepared for anything!

> *Char:* I remember when my kids were little we'd watch Barney the purple dinosaur on TV. I was always amazed at the oodles upon oodles of items that Barney would pull out of his "Barney bag." My tutoring tote is the same! It's chock-full of tutoring tools!!

One of the worst things that could happen is for you to show up for a tutoring session, the student has no homework, and you have nothing to do. Don't let this happen!

Go to your tutoring sessions prepared for anything!

Always carrying a bag full of school items and different mediums that help your tutoring sessions.

We highly recommend you bring a bag, backpack, portfolio, or something that you can carry materials in. Within that case should be tools of the trade, different learning tools, and extra items that the student might need to complete their schoolwork (reading material at the student's level, etc.).

Here are some ideas:

- Extra paper – Also, be sure to have three lined paper for handwriting practice

- Extra pen, pencils and pencil sharpener

- Extra erasers and ruler

- Small dry erase board with dry erase markers

- Small chalkboard with chalk pencils

- Reading material at different reading levels for each of your students

- An expandable folder with a pocket for each student where you can keep individualized notes and lessons

- Calculator

- Dictionary

- Clipboard with notepad – students always think it's cool to work on a clipboard!

- Flash cards or math props

- Wet wipes

- List of transition words and transition phrases for writing assignments

It's important to note that you should always have your calendar updated and with you. This can be on your smart phone or in paper form but when parents want to schedule or reschedule a lesson, you should be ready on the spot to accommodate! Making appointments is how you earn money.

It should be easy for parents to book appointments with you.

A smartphone or tablet with a data plan is a must. The students that you will be tutoring are digital natives. These are the kids that played with iPads as toddlers. Using your smartphone as a tool, rather than a toy, models its usefulness and the ease of research.

Remember, you want to pass on a love of learning to your students. Making learning fun and easy is what they long for. Most of our students don't want to learn or research, but when we pull out our phones and use them for tools, they are open and willing. Also, when internet and Wi-Fi aren't working you should always be able to use a hotspot on your phone to connect to your computer or your student's. Additional data is not very expensive when you consider your hourly pay.

Of course, you never want to hand a child a device that is connected to the internet without your supervision.

Always respect the trust that your student's parents have instilled in you.

Another tip that will help you with organizing your students is to keep a notebook for record-keeping.

A small composition book is the perfect size to keep your notes on who and what you tutor each day. For each tutoring session, write the date, time, the student's name, along with what you tutored that day. You can use this to recap your session with your student's parents and record your hours as well.

For Example:

1/15/2020   3:00-4:30

Johnny

> Reviewed Math Test, Completed Math Homework p.123
>
> Edited Rough Draft for History Paper
>
> Studied for Vocab Quiz on Friday

Taking the time to record the details of your tutoring session will help you on many levels.   It will provide an outline to show parents what material you covered as well as help you verify your hours for billing purposes. Additionally, the summary of your lessons can help you as you prepare for your next session with each student.   Sometimes when you have multiple students, remembering the lesson that you did last week can be mind boggling!

Lastly, don't be hesitant to make a financial investment to ensure that your tutoring sessions are fun and productive.

Buying additional data on your smartphone, or an educational toy that enhances learning for your student is just smart business!

> *Char:* Not long ago, one of my students, unbeknownst to me, was held out of school due to extended family visiting in town. When he showed up for his tutoring session, he had no papers, pencils, or backpack. But... I was prepared!

Phew!! I had the study guide for his math curriculum on my computer, and we were able to have a very productive tutoring session. Did I forget to mention that I put my laptop in my bag?! If you don't have a laptop, pack a tablet or have worksheets ready for those empty time slots.

Tutor Tip:

Go to your tutoring sessions prepared for anything!

Bring extra supplies and curricula

Let's Tutor!

Let's Tutor

What a Tutoring Session Looks Like

Okay, hold your horses - this is worth the price of this book! The single most important aspect to your successful tutoring business is:

Relationship, relationship, relationship!

Without establishing a good relationship with your student, you don't have much hope. With a good strong working relationship, in which your student knows you have their back and believe in them - you've got the moon!

It all boils down to unconditional acceptance. Each child is unique, has their strengths and weaknesses, and more than anything wants to feel valued.

Any type of judgmental attitude on your part will not cultivate the right kind of relationship you're trying to develop with your student.

Strive to treat each child as if they were your own child. It works! When they make a mistake or aren't sure of how to work out a problem, be patient and nurturing.

It's important to never make your student feel as though they are inadequate.

By taking the time to invest in their confidence, you will see that they'll feel good about themselves even when they make mistakes. If they believe you are their biggest cheerleader, your student can risk making a mistake and learn from it.

When they see you as their ally, learning is almost a sure thing!

Now, let's clarify. There is no golden nugget in tutoring.

Kids are still kids. There are still other factors to consider. This isn't a popularity contest *(although it doesn't hurt)*. At the first opportunity, they will likely throw you under the bus to save themselves from their parents or teachers when they miss an assignment or get a poor grade. When this happens, and it will, don't be offended. It's not personal - they'd do it to any tutor - it's just survival.

But If your students love you and know you genuinely care about them - things will go a lot smoother for you, for them, and for their parents.

Time and time again, parents will ask their kids, "Do you like your tutor?" probably more than, "Is your tutor teaching you?" With that said, let's talk about how to build the relationship.

Encourage –

Be sure to always take the opportunity to encourage your students. When you see them trying hard, mention it. When you see they want to give up...tell them you know they can do it.

Remain Calm –

When your student is acting up it's probably because they don't want to do the work. And quite likely because they don't understand what/how to accomplish the task before them. If you work with the same student for any length of time, they will test your patience.

Never lose your cool! Never! Ever! Losing your patience will put you in opposition with them.

Remember you are there to help them push through those frustrations and lack of confidence. If you lose your patience, they will lose their confidence. Take a deep breath and regroup silently.

Pray, ask God for wisdom. He gives it. Sometimes you will need to give your student a break while you formulate a strategy to help them. Remember the goal is always to help your student.

Model a Love of Learning –

Let's be honest, with much of tutoring you are having to relearn material. Even if you aren't, hopefully, you are tutoring a subject you enjoy. Let your students see how excited you are to learn a new fact or see how cool it is that the area of a triangle is half of a rectangle.

Teach your students tips and tricks.

When your student figures out the answer to a math problem in an unconventional way… get excited for him! Get him to teach you how he did it! Your student gets excited when he sees you are excited. It's doubtful they're going to get excited if you aren't!

Touching –

Touching your students needs to be handled very delicately. When in doubt… Don't touch. As a general rule, we high-five or fist bump. If there's any affection it's typically done in front of the parent.

You always want to maintain integrity and never raise any eyebrows or questions in your parent's mind. This is another good reason to tutor in public places. When you're in the student's home it's a good idea to be in a room where others can see you.

Also, understand with different cultures there are different boundaries. Be sure to take a little time and understand the boundaries in the culture that you are tutoring- or simply keep the atmosphere friendly (at a distance) and maintain mutual respect.

Relationship

The Single Most Important Element in your Tutoring

Understanding Learning Styles

Char: When I pursued my Masters degree, one of our assignments was to research whether or not students have different learning styles. A learning style is the method by which a particular person learns most comfortably. According to research, the jury is still out as to whether people favor a particular learning style over another.

As a parents and educators, Karen and I firmly believe that each of us has a "bent" and can/will learn more easily in one of the three main, "Learning Styles."

So, let's talk about the most common ways students learn.

There's something to be gained by understanding different methods of learning.

We've all had students lose interest in a lesson – or reach his limit before the lesson is over (i.e., his brain is fried). This information will help you understand different approaches to re-engage your learner.

The three most common ways that students learn is Visually, Kinesthetically, and Auditorily. Each of these types of learners are described for you below.

Can you find your students in any of these categories? Can you see yourself?

The Visual Learner

This student is sometimes called the spatial learner.

The visual or spatial learner is the one who learns most comfortably when he can see the lesson. This may include images, pictures, text, or the black/whiteboard. Because this learner can visualize things in his head, he is often good at interpreting charts, graphs, and even directions.

It may be difficult for him to follow along with the lecture-based class and you might notice him doodling on his paper because he finds it difficult to follow an auditory lesson.

Tips for a visual learner:

- Have him/her take notes during a lecture
- Drawing appropriate pictures can help them to understand a lesson
- Utilize picture mnemonics when teaching
- Assign them to take notes on the board, paper, or another medium, as the lesson is being taught
- Use visual aids (pictures, graphs, etc.) to reinforce teaching points
- Create mind maps to outline ideas

Clues that your student might be a visual learner:

- He enjoys the visual arts.

- He is creative.

- He says phrases like: "I can't picture it."

- He enjoys projects that he can see and is good at visualizing what he hears or reads.

- He easily reads and interprets maps and charts.

The Tactile/Kinesthetic Learner

The tactile learner is sometimes called the kinesthetic learner and is best known for their love of touching and exploring things.

They love building blocks, creating tents out of sheets, cooking, making project boards, etc. If they can touch the lesson and feel the lesson they are more likely to remember the information. Hands-on, or Project Based Learning, is their best friend.

Manipulatives are wonderful tools to use with this type of learner. They like to take things apart and see how an item works rather than read the diagram in the book.

This student would much rather build a project than write a book report. Often the traditional classroom setting is a challenge for a tactile learner.

Tips for a kinesthetic learner:

- Use flashcards to teach facts. Let them quiz you!

- Give regular breaks

- Create a game using the information or have *them* create a game with the info!

- Find a computer program that caters to what they need to study

- Act out scenes from history to reinforce a lesson

- Write or draw the lesson out

- Allow him to use a highlighter to highlight pertinent information while studying

- Have the students do jumping jacks and push-ups to break up long study sessions

Clues that your student might be a kinesthetic learner:

- Learns best through hands-on activities

- Readily engages in activities and remembers the details taught in the process

- Enjoys teamwork

- Thinks quickly

The Auditory Learner

An Auditory learner most easily learns by listening and talking. They are able to retain information that they hear easier than their classmates that favor other learning styles.

Putting facts to music helps this type of learner learn very quickly. Learning a math formula or a continent full of countries can be daunting! Introducing a rhyme, music, or mnemonics into the lesson can expedite the learning process for the auditory student. Reading aloud and repetition are instrumental in order for them to retain information. Even soft music with this type of learner can help in their learning environment.

You might notice that often these students are gifted at singing or playing instruments or have a natural sense of rhythm. They also typically hold conversations with adults very comfortably.

Auditory learners enjoy group discussions, interactive activities and debates. Reading silently may be a difficult task for this student.

Tips for an auditory learner:

- Break up test taking sessions

- Tap out rhythms or create jingles or mnemonics for memorization

- Brainstorm study sessions with back-and-forth questions and answers. Allow your student to be the teacher and teach you. Hearing his own voice can help him learn quicker.

- Be sure to have him read the instructions out loud to any assignments.

Clues that your student might be an auditory learner:

- Retains information from lectures

- Understands directions

- Comprehends text much better when it's read aloud vs. read silently

Char: One day I was teaching a history lesson to a strong auditory/tactile learner, he began drawing a floor plan of his new house. Privately, I wondered if he could really be listening while sketching a floor plan. I gave him the benefit of the doubt and continued teaching the lesson without pause. About that same time, his cousin (who I was also tutoring) saw what he was doing and she thought she would also draw. *Whoa!* I knew without a doubt - she could not listen and draw simultaneously! As you can imagine, she wasn't very happy when I asked her to pay attention. She argued and insisted that she was listening just like her cousin (*"If he can, I can too!"*) That's where the rubber met the road. I asked her a comprehension question about the material I had been presenting... busted! She couldn't answer. Between you and me... I was a little nervous when I asked her cousin a similar question but thankfully he quickly responded with the correct answer! It is extremely beneficial to be sensitive to your student's learning styles.

Understanding the different learning styles will help you become a better tutor.

You'll find that when you tutor a single subject for long periods of time, your student will often zone out. When this happens, you'll need to think quickly as to how handle it. Keep in mind the different learning styles and switch things up a bit.

Review the tips from each learning style and pick what will help your student push through tough times.

Unfortunately, as a tutor your time is limited - so, there isn't time to waste in a session. Making the most of your tutoring time and finding the method that works best with your student requires you to be creative!

Often when you tutor math for more than 20-30 minutes students will show signs of brain fatigue. At that point, have them walk around, do some jumping jacks, talk about their weekend plans, or pull out a dry erase board – and then try again. You can even use tile floor to help you calculate the area of a space! Again, be creative - you students will love it!

Switching up the learning style works nine out of ten times to regain your student's attention.

Many times, just having your student move around and then switching to a dry erase board is magical!

Karen: I tutor a delightful girl for 3 hours at a time, twice each week. She is homeschooled and her mother wanted me to help her with three of her subjects. Three hours is a long time, and I have to change things up frequently to keep that fatigue from setting in. A few years ago, when she was learning to write, we would go outside and practice writing letters of the alphabet in the sandbox. For spelling, she would jump on the mini-trampoline while spelling out loud the words from her weekly list.

She is older now so we do mostly seat work at the dining room table or go to an outdoor patio table when the weather is nice, while stopping to take quick breaks as often as necessary.

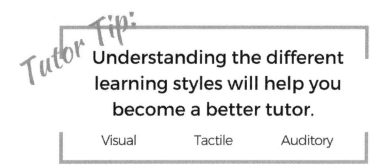

Tutor Tip: **Understanding the different learning styles will help you become a better tutor.**

| Visual | Tactile | Auditory |

Keeping Communication Open with Parents

Keeping the lines of communication open with your student's parents is vital. As a tutor, you should genuinely appreciate the opportunity to work with your students.

It is a great honor that your student's parents trust you with their children.

Part of earning that trust is keeping the communication open with parents.

For each tutoring session, it's smart to keep a notebook in which you write details about what you covered in your session. Be sure to take that notebook to every appointment and fill it in as you tutor.

In addition to your notebook, you can provide a three-ring binder that you leave at your student's house - with a summary sheet describing your tutoring session, the date, work covered, and also the actual work you completed that is extra-curricular beyond their homework.

At the end of every session, be sure to connect with the parents and let them know what material was covered during your tutoring session - and if there needs to be any follow up assignments completed.

This reassures the parents that their child has been making best use of your tutoring time and also assures them that you have their child's best interest at heart.

Connecting with the parents will allow you to voice any concerns, observations, or homework that needs to be addressed.

During these quick parent-tutor meetings at the end of your tutoring sessions, take the opportunity to talk about the strengths and concerns that you see in their child.

Don't miss a chance to praise the student when you see their strengths! This reinforces good character and helps to establish (both to the parent and the student), that you enjoy working with your student.

Surprisingly, some parents will just drop off and pick up their students and never make a point to connect with you. Their level of trust is amazing! With those parents, be sure to connect with them via email, text or a phone call.

It only takes a minute to type a quick text to let them know the material you covered and how their child did. Sending them a text/ email recapping what you did, along with any positive comments you can make will help the drop-off parents appreciate their investment in tutoring for their child.

Having a tutoring session template to print out and complete during each tutoring appointment is a smart idea. A tutoring session form would detail the subjects and material you covered, as well as homework that the student needs to complete. There should also be a section for notes or comments in which you can inform the parents of upcoming tests or how the student performed in the session. We have provided two different templates you can print out on our website (www.gatewaytotutoring.com). You can view them in the Resource section of this book.

Remember that parents see you as an expert.

Take that role seriously and advise the parents on your observations, experiences and concerns. Be sure to always end on a positive note.

It is important to regularly convey to a parent the positive qualities you see in their child.

Parents are naturally interested in your observations. When they see that you care, parents will be more likely to hear you (without defense) when you need to address them with a concern.

In turn, when you encourage the child to work out of their comfort zone, the parent(s) are more likely to be supportive. Mom and Dad know when you are genuine and have their child's best interest at heart.

Tutor Tip:

Be sure to always end on a positive note

Remember that parents see you as an expert. Take that role seriously, and share your observations.

Connecting with the Student's School

When you have a regular student, that has specific struggles, it is a good idea to connect with their teacher at school. This may mean sending an email to introduce yourself or setting up an in-class meeting. Being available to do this will set you apart from other tutors.

Stepping out beyond your tutoring session to help your student sends a message to the parents that you genuinely care about the future and the trajectory of their child's education.

If your client tells you about a parent-teacher conference that is scheduled, you may want to offer to attend the meeting. Be sure to relay to the parents your desire to collaborate with the teachers in order to be as effective as possible in your tutoring sessions with their child. Attending a parent-teacher conference will allow you the opportunity to hear firsthand the teachers concerns. This will help you focus on areas with your student that you may not otherwise be aware of.

Char: In one parent teacher conference that I attended I found out that my student had accommodations - which I had no idea about previously! I was able to get a copy of the accommodations and focus on areas that were detailed in his IEP (Individualized Education Program).

If you don't have the opportunity to meet your student's teacher firsthand, you may want to send an email introducing yourself and ask the teacher how you can be most helpful, what areas of concern they have, and where they would like to see your student progress.

Be sure to take the time to create a professional signature line for your email before you introduce yourself. If you're not sure what a professional signature line looks like for a tutor, search *"professional email signature tutor"* on the internet and you will find many examples. Create one for yourself. These little details help to reinforce that you are a professional.

Parents always appreciate your attentiveness to their child, especially when they see that you are willing to be an advocate for them. Who doesn't like a little help!?

After you establish a relationship of respect with the parents, offer to be an advocate for them if you notice that they have concerns with the school, curriculum, or teacher.

As a tutor, you have a unique position that allows you to ask for information and details that the parents may not be able to get.

When you do ask for information from the teacher/schools be sure to ask with a tone of "expecting" rather than "asking if they could do such and such."

Every correspondence with the teacher/school should include your student's parents in the email "CC:"

Here are some suggestions to include an email to the teacher/school:

- Introduce yourself as the student's tutor and express your desire to come alongside the teacher so that the student arrives to their class prepared and confident.

- Let the teacher know the days of the week you tutor the student (every day, on Wednesdays, etc.).

- Let them know you are aware of the curriculum – if you have a copy of the curriculum, let the teacher know this, as it makes it easier to communicate regarding lessons.

- Ask the teacher their areas of concern that you can focus on, so that your time with the student is as productive and effective as possible.

- Express your observations and ask the teacher if your observations are what they have experienced. For example: "I've noticed that Johnny memorizes the math formulas and forgets them quickly because he doesn't understand the concepts," or "Emily has strong oratory skills and can summarize a story verbally but can't seem to translate it into a written format," etc.

- Offer your assistance and availability to meet the teacher (if the student is a regular student).

- Keep the tone professional and friendly. You never want a teacher to feel threatened or judged by your being involved in his/her student's life.

As a tutor, it is easy to draw conclusions regarding teachers and their inadequacies as you tutor their students – especially with the students that you tutor frequently.

Students will tell you stories about their teachers and what the teacher's expectations are, how they grade, how they test, etc.

However, it's important to understand that you don't have the full picture and are receiving information about that teacher - from a biased child.

Teachers have a tough job. As a tutor, you have the opportunity to come alongside them and make their jobs easier.

Undoubtedly, you will run across a teacher that isn't teaching in a way you wish they would.

Nonetheless, it is vitally important to respect their role in our student's life.

Never, ever badmouth a teacher. They are in a position of authority. It's important to remember that we are privileged to work one-on-one with our students, and in doing so, we can help to mold their character (which is far more important than their education).

Being under a "challenging" teacher can help to build character and patience in our students, if we come alongside them and teach them to respect the teacher (good or bad).

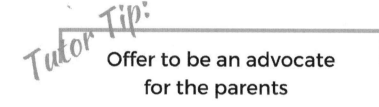

Offer to be an advocate for the parents

To address concerns they have with the school, curriculum, or teacher.

Practical Tips for Your Time Together

First and foremost, be friendly. You don't want to portray yourself as another grumpy teacher. You want to walk the tightrope between teacher and friend. It's a delicate balance.

Your student should see you as someone who is their advocate. You expect them to perform and complete their work, but you are on their side. (For the most part!) There is a balance because ultimately you are working for their parents, and while you can "cover for them" a little, you can't do it too much.

The parents of your student are spending good money for your services. It is important to use every minute wisely.

Make sure you are ready to dig-in the moment you get started on a session. Trust us, the parent who hired you will notice and appreciate it. Occasionally a sibling or other family member will interject comments and try to start conversations if they happen to be passing by… "Oh, I remember when the Berlin Wall fell. I even visited it once!" Sometimes a short conversation can actually add value to the lesson, but if you notice it getting off onto other topics, politely resume what you were working on with the student. You might look at the student and say something like, "Oh look, we only have 30 more minutes and still need to cover the material for your math quiz tomorrow." It always works and no one is offended. If you don't have to leave immediately after you are done, you may continue that conversation with the family member afterwards.

A helpful tool to break up sessions – when you don't have time for a break - is a brain teaser, a fun riddle or a joke. These can take as little as one minute and will help to break up the monotony of a challenging topic. They also help to clear your student's mind from being overwhelmed and allow you to continue on with your lesson.

Tutor Tip:

Watch The Clock

Be respectful of the time and
use it wisely

Going the Extra Mile

We all appreciate someone who goes the extra mile, and you can be that person for your clients. Extending common courtesy and frequent communication is a great beginning.

Here are additional ideas that will help you to stand out from other tutors:

- Return correspondence promptly

- Be one step ahead

- Be available to help even when you're off the clock

- Research learning disabilities that you see in your students to understand the best way to help them learn

- Be flexible in scheduling

- Be constantly looking for resources or books that can enhance your student's learning

Karen: One of my students was working on a unit study about birds in which she took immense delight. I found a wonderful book which gave descriptions and vocalizations of 75 bird species across the eastern United States where she lives. I gave it to her as a gift one day, and boy was it a hit! I love giving that little extra which enhances a child's learning and brings them joy. Another one of my students had shown interest in making electronic gadgets, so on his birthday I gifted him with a simple electronics kit. He loved it!

Remembering birthdays is always appreciated. In addition, you may also want to attend an occasional event in which your student is involved such as concerts, soccer games, and theater productions.

Tutor Tip:

Going the Extra Mile

Will set you apart from other tutors

Gaps in Your Students' Knowledge

A learning gap is the difference between what a student knows and what they are expected to have learned at a certain point in their education. As a tutor, it's important to identify those gaps and fill them in - which can be a daunting task. Don't worry about getting a complete assessment of what level your student is at right away. Many of the learning deficits will rise to the surface as you work through material.

Here are two ways to get you started:

Ask –

Begin the session by asking the student to tell you what they know about the subject at hand. This helps not only to grasp an overall sense of where the student is at, but also allows you to correct any misconceptions.

Test –

There are many assessments available which touch on the rudiments of a subject for a particular grade level. Personally, we only administer these if we suspect there are gaps present. These are extremely helpful when trying to get a child "caught-up." Being able to identify your student's weaknesses and addressing them will help to fill in those learning gaps.

If, and when, weaknesses are identified, it's helpful to split your tutoring sessions into two parts.

Initially, focus on the current assignments that the student is working on so they do not fall behind on their work.

Afterwards, work on material that they have not mastered but should have at this point. Make a point to allow at least 15 minutes for this - if you can.

For example, if a student has not mastered fractions, you could have a worksheet where you teach converting mixed fractions to improper fractions and vice versa. In reading, you can spend time reading a short passage from a good book and then spend a few minutes identifying the nouns, prepositions, and the like.

We have found that using this sequence: current schoolwork and then review, works best for the majority of our students. Even doing five to ten minutes of "warm-up" exercises could be enough review for your student to remember the new concepts.

We recommend that whenever you start a new subject or new

concept: don't assume your student knows the basics. Rather, start with the rudimentary information first and build from there. This will help to build their confidence as you introduce the more challenging concepts.

For example, when discussing the space race, you may ask the student to point out where the Soviet Union was on a map, tell what main country was it comprised of, explain the Cold War, etc. This background information is important in understanding the effect the original Sputnik had on Americans back in 1957. As you talk through the material, ask questions to find where there are gaps in knowledge. This is critical, especially in subjects such as math and science where learning is built upon what has been mastered previously.

If there is a knowledge deficit, spending some time bringing the child up to speed is warranted before continuing.

We sometimes will just call a 'quick review' before tackling the homework assignment, and that way the student doesn't feel embarrassed or frustrated by being quizzed.

If understanding is there, then great, you are ready to plow into the new material.

Karen: A couple of years ago I began teaching a new student and we were reviewing marine science. He was 11 years old and we were discussing the characteristics of sharks. I described how a shark's skin has denticles and feels like sandpaper if he were to touch it. I went on with other similar animals with that type of skin texture, such as rays. As I spoke, I noticed he was looking at me with puzzlement and asked, "What is sandpaper?" I was surprised that a child his age was not acquainted with sandpaper. Not reacting in any way, as to not to embarrass him, I explained what it was and at the next session I brought some sandpaper from home for him to look at and feel. We spent a few minutes discussing what it is used for.

Realize that not everyone has had the same exposure or opportunities that you or your children have had.

This leads us to the concept of "The Curse of Knowledge" in a larger sense.

It's easy and natural to think that just because something is obvious to you, it must be obvious to the student.

For example, in 1990 a Harvard graduate student, Elizabeth Newton, conducted a study in which one group of participants were asked to tap out a well-known song. The tappers always overestimated the percentage of people listening who could figure out the song. Just imagine tapping out "Jingle Bells" as the song is playing in your head. It may be obvious to you, yet it was proven that the listener was rarely able to identify the correct song.

Be mindful of your own "Curse of Knowledge."

That is, just because you know something that is obvious to you, does not mean your student knows it as well.

Try to put yourself in the position of your student as if you're learning something for the first time. This is very challenging and in doing so, it requires an attentiveness to your student. We call it being a "student of your student."

> *Karen*: The curse of knowledge is very much on my mind when I teach math. I have worked with math for so long that I intuitively know much of the material.
>
> I have to remind myself that just because it seems like second nature to me, it may not make sense to students who are seeing it for the first time. I try and put myself in my student's shoes.

Look for clues that you student may not truly understand the material when he is saying, "Yeah, I get it," to. He can be hesitant or quiet. These are typical behaviors that students exhibit when they are less confident or lost. Knowing this will help you be aware of how much of the material your student is retaining.

Lastly, use concrete examples and stories to illustrate concepts. That's the best way to make the material stick.

Tutor Tip:

Be mindful of your own "Curse of Knowledge"

Just because you know something that is obvious to you...
Does not mean your student knows it as well

Conclusion

Whether you're still in school, just graduated, raising a family, looking for extra income, or wanting to use your years of experience to help others and make money... *TUTORING IS FOR YOU!*

Tutoring is a business that allows you to name your price, your hours and your investment with amazing returns!

Are you tired of a mundane or meaningless job?

> *Tutoring allows you to impact lives and inspire others.*

Do you want to be your own boss?

> *You can work as much or as little as you'd like.*

Would you like the freedom to schedule your own hours and name your price?

> *You can work mornings, afternoons, or evenings. Weekend tutors are needed as well.*

> *You set your price and your availability.*

Do you have a desire to change the world - one student at a time?

> *There are no words to describe the satisfaction of knowing that your investment in a student helped equip them to be all that they were created to be. Inspiring confidence and a love of learning in our students is the fuel that keeps us going!*

Tutoring is a business you can start as a side hustle or a full-time career.

If these are goals you are hoping to achieve – you can start tutoring tomorrow!

For more information or to connect with us - you can find us at GatewaytoTutoring.com.

We love helping people and we'd love to hear how you're doing!

Resources for Tutors

All resources are in printable pdf form for you to download and use by means of our website:

www.GatewaytoTutoring.com

<u>Parent Questionnaire:</u>

PARENT QUESTIONNAIRE

Student's Name: _____ Date: _____

Birthdate: _____ School: _____ Grade: _____

Parent's Name: Mother: _____ Father: _____

Address: _____

Phone Number _____ Your Email _____

1. Please list your child's strengths (e.g. very organized, thorough, motivated, etc.) _____

2. Please list the opportunities for improvement that your child has as a student. (e.g. struggles w/ organization, lack of confidence, reading comprehension, etc.) _____

3. What is/are the reason(s) you would like your child to be tutored? Please explain any concerns you have: _____

4. Have school teachers or counselors expressed concern about your child's performance? _____ If yes, please explain. _____

5. List any special interests your child has. This can assist me to establish rapport and find books/articles with subjects that appeal to your child. (e.g. plays violin, sports) _____

6. Does your child have accommodations at school or an IEP? _____ If yes, please explain _____

7. Is your child receiving any special help at school, such as tutoring/reading assistance? _____ If yes, please explain. _____

8. What are your goals for your child? _____

Is there any other information you'd like me to know about your child? _____

Thank you! I look forward to working together to inspire your child to love learning.
WWW.GATEWAYTOTUTORING.COM

Student Survey:

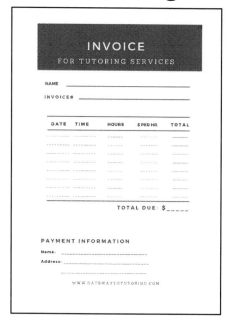

STUDENT SURVEY

Your Name: _____   Date: _____

Birthdate: _____ School: _____ Grade: ____

1. What are your strengths? What are you really good at? (e.g. very organized, thorough, motivated, etc.)
....

2. What are some things that don't come easy to you? (e.g. struggle w/organization, math, lack of confidence, reading comprehension, etc.)
....

3. What things do you like to do when you're not in school? Hobbies/interests? Do you like to read about any of those things?
....

4. What do you like to read about? What type of books do you like to read?
....

5. What do you like best about school? Why? Anything you don't like? Why?
....

6. List any special interests you have. (e.g. playing violin, soccer, drawing, singing, etc.)
....

7. Are you receiving tutoring or reading assistance at school? _____ If yes, What kind?
....

8. Do you have any goals that I can help you with? _____

9. Is there anything else you might like me to know?
....

Thank you! I look forward to working with you!

WWW.GATEWAYTOTUTORING.COM

Invoice for Tutoring Session:

INVOICE
FOR TUTORING SERVICES

NAME _____

INVOICE# _____

DATE	TIME	HOURS	$ PER HR.	TOTAL
....	....	....	....	....
....	....	....	....	....
....	....	....	....	....
....	....	....	....	....
....	....	....	....	....
....	....	....	....	....

TOTAL DUE: $ _ _ _ _ _

PAYMENT INFORMATION

Name: _____

Address: _____

WWW.GATEWAYTOTUTORING.COM

Tutoring Session Summaries:

Sample 1

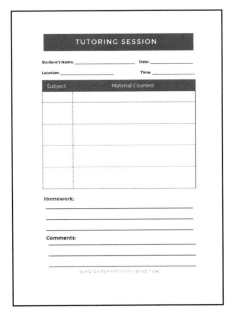

Sample 2

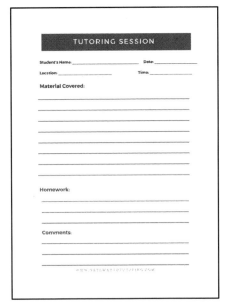

More resources can be found at www.GatewayToTutoring.com as we add them on. We welcome suggestions for forms you may need.

Made in the USA
San Bernardino, CA
03 April 2019